Pebble® Plus

Presidents' Day

FEBRUARY

by Clara Cella

Consulting Editor: Gail Saunders-Smith, PhD

CAPSTONE PRESS
a capstone imprint

Pebble Plus is published by Capstone Press,
1710 Roe Crest Drive, North Mankato, Minnesota 56003.
www.capstonepub.com

Library of Congress Cataloging-in-Publication Data
Cella, Clara.
Presidents' Day / by Clara Cella.
p. cm. — (Pebble plus. Let's celebrate)
Includes index.
Summary: "Full-color photographs and simple text provide a brief introduction to Presidents' Day"—Provided
by publisher.
ISBN 978-1-4296-8734-8 (library binding)
ISBN 978-1-4296-9392-9 (paperback)
ISBN 978-1-62065-309-8 (ebook PDF)
1. Presidents' Day—Juvenile literature. 2. Presidents—United States—History—Juvenile literature. I. Title.

E176.8.C45 2013
394.261—dc23   2012003824

Editorial Credits
Jill Kalz, editor; Kyle Grenz, designer; Marcie Spence, media researcher; Kathy McColley, production specialist

Photo Credits
Capstone Studio: Karon Dubke, 7, 21, 22; iStockphoto: Kubrak78, 17; Library of Congress, 11; Shutterstock: fotoGN,
15, fstockfoto, cover (Mt. Rushmore), gary yim, 5, imagedj, cover (White House), Samuel Acosta, 1, Tischenko
Irina, cover (flag), Vacclav, 9, Victorian Traditions, 13, ZouZou, 19

Note to Parents and Teachers

The Let's Celebrate series supports curriculum standards for social studies related to culture.
This book describes and illustrates the Presidents' Day holiday. The images support early
readers in understanding the text. The repetition of words and phrases helps early readers
learn new words. This book also introduces early readers to subject-specific vocabulary words,
which are defined in the Glossary section. Early readers may need assistance to read some
words and to use the Table of Contents, Glossary, Read More, Internet Sites, and Index
sections of the book.

Printed in the United States of America in North Mankato, Minnesota.
042012   006682CGF12

Table of Contents

Hello, Presidents' Day!. 4

How It Began. 10

Let's Celebrate! 16

Activity: Dear President 22

Read More 23

Internet Sites. 23

Glossary 24

Index 24

Hello, Presidents' Day!

Presidents' Day is a time

to honor U.S. presidents.

Americans remember

their country's history

and its leaders.

Presidents' Day is

on the third Monday of February.

It is a national holiday.

Government offices and

schools are closed that day.

7

Being president is a hard job.

On Presidents' Day

Americans honor the work

their presidents have done.

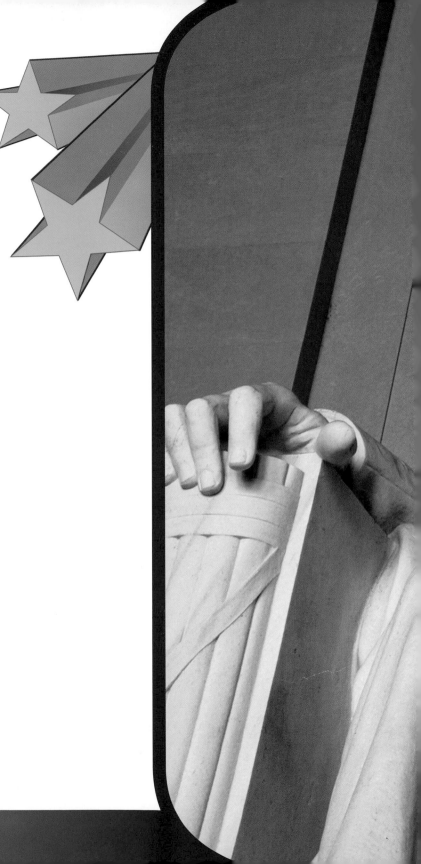

FOR WHOM HE SAVED THE UNION
THE MEMORY OF ABRAHAM LINCOLN
IS ENSHRINED FOREVER

9

How It Began

Presidents' Day began

as two holidays celebrating

George Washington's and

Abraham Lincoln's birthdays.

Both men were brave presidents.

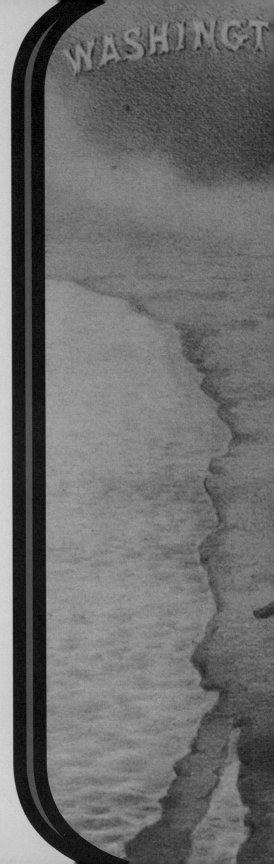

11

Washington was a leader
during the Revolutionary War
(1775–1783). He became the first
U.S. president. Lincoln was president
during the Civil War (1861–1865).

George Washington crossing the Delaware River, 1776

Americans first celebrated

Presidents' Day in 1968.

It soon became a time to honor

all U.S. presidents, not just

Washington and Lincoln.

Jefferson Memorial, Washington, D.C.

Let's Celebrate!

It's Presidents' Day!

How will you celebrate?

Read books about U.S. presidents.

Visit a president's monument

in person or on the Internet.

Visitor Center
Amphitheater
Presidential Trail
Sculptor's Studio

Make a list. What do you think
makes a good president?
Good listening skills? Strength?
Being smart? Being friendly?

19

Fill your classroom

with red, white, and blue.

Fly a U.S. flag. Or draw your own!

Write a story about you

becoming the next president.

Activity: Dear President

Ask a question or share your thoughts with the president.

What You Need:

paper

a pen

an envelope

a first-class stamp

What You Do:

1. Write your address, the date, and the president's address at the top of the letter. Below it write "Dear President _____."

2. Start by saying who you are. Say why you're writing.

3. End by thanking the president for reading your letter. Then sign your name.

4. Write the president's address on the center of the envelope.

   The President of the United States

   The White House

   1600 Pennsylvania Avenue NW

   Washington, D.C. 20500

5. Write your address in the upper-left corner.

6. Put a stamp in the upper-right corner.

7. Drop the envelope in the mail and wait for a reply!

Read More

Dayton, Connor. *Presidents' Day.* American Holidays. New York: PowerKids Press, 2012.

Peppas, Lynn. *Presidents' Day.* Celebrations in My World. New York: Crabtree Pub., 2010.

Rissman, Rebecca. *Presidents' Day.* Holidays and Festivals. Chicago: Heinemann Library, 2011.

Internet Sites

FactHound offers a safe, fun way to find Internet sites related to this book. All of the sites on FactHound have been researched by our staff.

Here's all you do:

Visit *www.facthound.com*

Type in this code: 9781429687348

Check out projects, games and lots more at
www.capstonekids.com

Glossary

celebrate—to honor someone or something on a special day

Civil War—(1861–1865) the battle between states in the North and South that led to the end of slavery in the United States

monument—a statue or building that is meant to remind people of an event or a person

Revolutionary War—(1775–1783) the American Colonies' fight for freedom from Great Britain

Index

activities, 16, 18, 20

closings, 6

dates, 6

history of holiday, 10, 14

honoring, 4, 8, 14

Lincoln, Abraham, 10, 12, 14

monuments, 16

Washington, George, 10, 12, 14

Word Count: 187
Grade: 1
Early-Intervention Level: 21